My Family

Adoptive Families

by Sarah L. Schuette

Consulting Editor: Gail Saunders-Smith, PhD

CAPSTONE PRESS
a capstone imprint

Pebble Books are published by Capstone Press,
151 Good Counsel Drive, P.O. Box 669, Mankato, Minnesota 56002.
www.capstonepress.com

Printed in the United States of America in North Mankato, Minnesota
092009
005618CGS10

 Books published by Capstone Press are manufactured with paper containing at least 10 percent post-consumer waste.

Library of Congress Cataloging-in-Publication Data
Schuette, Sarah L., 1976–
    Adoptive families / by Sarah L. Schuette.
    p. cm. — (Pebble books. My family)
    Includes bibliographical references and index.
    Summary: "Simple text and photographs present adoptive families, including how family members interact with one another" — Provided by publisher.
    ISBN 978-1-4296-3977-4 (library binding)
    ISBN 978-1-4296-4836-3 (paperback)
    1. Adoption — Juvenile literature. 2. Adoptive parents — Juvenile literature. I. Title. II. Series.
HV875.S367 2010
306.874 — dc22   2009023381

Note to Parents and Teachers

The My Family set supports national social studies standards related to identifying family members and their roles in the family. This book describes and illustrates adoptive families. The images support early readers in understanding the text. The repetition of words and phrases helps early readers learn new words. This book also introduces early readers to subject-specific vocabulary words, which are defined in the Glossary section. Early readers may need assistance to read some words and to use the Table of Contents, Glossary, Read More, Internet Sites, and Index sections of the book.

Table of Contents

4

About Adoptive Families

Some parents adopt children born to other people. These parents and children make up adoptive families.

adoptive father

adopted daughter

adoptive mother

Adopted children
are legal members
of their new family.

Siblings and other
family members are also
part of adoptive families.

Helping

Adoptive family members
help each other.
Nate helps his dad
by feeding the dog.

12

Patty helps her father
do laundry.

Tony's mother teaches him
to play piano.

Having Fun

Adopted family members
have fun together.
Kyle and his grandmother
play dominoes.

Vera and her sister
bake a cake.

Adoptive family members love each other.

Glossary

adopt — to make a child a legal member of a family

dominoes — a game played with tiles that have numbered dots on them

grandmother — the mother of your mother or father

laundry — clothes, towels, sheets, and other items that are washed to make them clean

legal — by law; adopted children are full members of a family by law.

member — a part of a group or family

parent — a mother or a father

sibling — a brother or a sister

Read More

Aubrey, Annette. *Flora's Family: Understanding Adoption.* QEB Understanding. Laguna Hills, Calif.: QEB Publishing, 2008.

Levete, Sarah. *Fostering and Adoption.* Let's Talk About. North Mankato, Minn.: Stargazer Books, 2007.

Rice, Beth. *I'm Adopted, I'm Special.* Sarasota, Fla.: Peppertree Press, 2008.

Internet Sites

FactHound offers a safe, fun way to find Internet sites related to this book. All of the sites on FactHound have been researched by our staff.

Here's all you do:

Visit *www.facthound.com*

FactHound will fetch the best sites for you!

Index

Word Count: 88
Grade: 1
Early-Intervention Level: 10

Editorial Credits
Gillia Olson, editor; Juliette Peters, designer; Sarah Schuette, photo stylist;
    Marcy Morin, studio scheduler; Eric Manske, production specialist

Photo Credits
All photos by Capstone Studio/Karon Dubke

The Capstone Press Photo Studio thanks Countryside Homes in Mankato, Minn.,
for its help with photo shoots for this book.

The author dedicates this book to her first friend, Jennifer Haar.